Android:

Programming and App Development for Beginners

By Samuel Shields

2nd Edition

the consent of the author or copyright owner. Legal action will be pursued if this is breached.

Disclaimer Notice:

Please note the information contained within this document is for educational and entertainment purposes only. Every attempt has been made to provide accurate, up to date and reliable complete information. No warranties of any kind are expressed or implied. Readers acknowledge that the author is not engaging in the rendering of legal, financial, medical or professional advice.

By reading this document, the reader agrees that under no circumstances are we responsible for any losses, direct or indirect, which are incurred as a result of the use of information contained within this document, including, but not limited to, —errors, omissions, or inaccuracies.

Contents

Introduction

Android is one of the most popular mobile operating systems in the world and the main reason for that is because it is open source. This means that the source code is available for anyone to look into and to modify for their own use. It is also a Linux-based operating system and is available on a wider range of tablets, phablets and smartphones than any other mobile operating system.

Android was developed by an organization called the *Open Handset Alliance,* an alliance that is led by Google and other major companies. In 2007, Google released the Android SDK (Software Development Kit) in beta form and this was followed in September 2008 by the very first commercial version of the operating system.

At this moment in time, Android is fast catching up to, if not about to take over iOS in terms of development options and, with more than one billion devices currently actively running Android across the globe today, it is the easiest place to make your mark as an app developer.

On top of that, Android's app provisioning and submission policy is much more open than any other mobile operating system and that means that it is much easier to get your app on the market pretty much straightaway. I will be talking later on in the book about how to develop your first app and what goes into it, to give you some idea of where to start.

So, if you have been thinking about developing an app and you have a good idea, delve in and get started.

Chapter 1 – Why Android?

Well, as I mentioned earlier, Android is the most popular operating system for mobile devices and is also a very powerful one. Its features include:

- A user-friendly and intuitive interface

- Numerous connections, including GSM/EDGE, Bluetooth, UMTS, Wi-Fi, WiMAX, LTE, CDMA and NFC

- Uses SQLite for storage purposes – SQLite is a relational database manager

- Full support for a wide range of media options, including BMP, GIF, JPEG, PNG, H.263, H.264, MPEG-4, AAC, MP3, MIDI and WAV to name just a few

- Supports both MMS and SMS messaging options

- The web browser supports both CSS3 and HTML5 and is based on the WebKit layout engine, which is open source and couple up with the V8 JavaScript engine from Chrome

- The screen supports multi-touch

- It's easy for users to multi-task, moving with ease from one task to another and running several applications at the same time

- It has resizable widgets that can be expanded or shrunk, depending on the user's preferences

- Has support for both single and bi-directional text

- It has GCM – Google Cloud Messaging – a service that allows developers to send short message data to Android users without needing a sync solution

- It supports Wi-Fi direct which allows apps to find and pair directly, using a high-bandwidth P2P connection

- It has Android Bean, which is NFC –based and it allows users to share content instantly, just by touching two devices with NFC together.

Android Applications

When you develop an Android application, it is usually done in the Java programming language together with the Android software development kit, which includes virtually everything you need to develop your app and get it to the market.

Your market is your choice. You can go for the Google Play Store, Opera Mobile store, Amazon App Store, Slide ME, Mobango, or F-Droid, to name but a few.

App Categories

There are hundreds of different categories for Android apps; the most difficult part for you is finding the one that your app is going to fit into. The top rated categories, and not in any particular order, are:

- Music

- Sports

- Travel

- Business

- Social media

- News

- Lifestyle

- Weather

- Reference

- Utilities

- Multimedia

- Food and Drink

- Boks

- Navigation

- Finance

Android Names

Each new version of Android is given a code name and they go in alphabetical order:

- Aestro

- Blender

- Cupcake 1.5

- Donut 1.6

- Éclair 2.0-2.1

- Froyo 2.2x

- Gingerbread 2.3x

- Honeycomb 3.x

- Ice Cream Sandwich 4.0x

- Jelly Bean 4.1x

- KitKat 4.4x

- Lollipop 5.0

You may be wondering why any of this is important to an app developer. When you start to write an app, you want to know what features are available on Android devices because it will affect what you can and can't do with the app. It is also important to know the different versions for the same reasons. Also, bear in mind that the earlier versions are not used as much so it isn't worth developing an app specifically for them. The same goes for Lollipop 5.0 – very few devices actually run this version at the moment so you would be severely limiting your range.

With the rest of this book, my intention is to teach you how to develop your app and, in the next chapter, I will start by talking about how to set your environment up.

Chapter 2 – Getting Started

Getting started with Android is quite simple and you can use any of the following systems to begin developing apps:

- Microsoft Windows XP or higher

- Mac OS X 1.5.8 or higher

- Linux, with GNU C Library 2.7 or higher

Everything you need to begin developing is available freely on the internet. You will need to download the following:

- Java Development Kit (JDK) 5 or higher

- Android Software Development Kit

- Java Runtime Environment (JRE) 6 or higher

- Android Studio

- Eclipse IDE For Java Developers

The last item on this list is optional but if you are using a Windows computer to develop your app, it will make things a little easier for you.

How to Set Up the Java Development Kit

Download the JDK from the above line and then follow the instructions given on the website for installing it – they are easy to follow. The next step is to set two environment variables, HOME and PATH, which refer to the directory containing Java and JavaC. These are usually found in java_instal_dir/bin and Java_install_dir respectively. If you are using a Windows PC, there are two ways to do this. The first is check where JDK is installed. Let's say that you installed in C:\jdk1.6.0_15 (your reference numbers will be different depending on the version you installed), you would need to open up C:\autoexec.bat and add in this line (again, make sure you use the right version numbers):

- set PATH=C:\jdk1.7.0_75\bin;%PATH%

- set JAVA_HOME=C:\jdk1.7.0_75

The second way is to right-click on **My Computer.** From the menu, choose **Properties** and then click on **Advanced System Settings**. Click on the System tab and them on

Environment Variables. Update the value for PATH and click on OK.

If you are using a Linux system and the SDK was installed in /usr/jdk1.6.0_15 and you are using C shell, you would need to open your .cshrc file and input this line:

- setenv PATH /usr/local/jdk1.7.0_75/bin:$PATH

- setenv JAVA_HOME /usr/local/jdk1.7.0_75

If you are using an Integrated Development Environment (IDE) Eclipse, it will already know where Java has been installed.

How Android is Configured

The Android operating system is a stack system made up of different components on four layers:

Linux Kernel

Right at the bottom of the stack is Linux, containing more than 100 patches. This is where the device hardware drivers are stores, such as the drivers needed for the keypad, camera and the display for example. The Linux kernel is also tasked with handling everything that Linux excels at, like networking and all the device drivers. This takes the sting out of having to interface with peripheral hardware

Libraries

Above the Linux kernel are the libraries. Included in these are the WebKit engine for the web browser, lib, which is a well-known library, the SQLite database for storing and share data, libraries need to record and play audio and video files, and the libraries that are responsible for security on the internet, to name just a few of the many that are there.

Android Libraries

Next up are the Android libraries, which hold the Java libraries needed for Android development. In here, you would find things like the application framework libraries a well as those that help the user with building an interface, drawing graphics and accessing databases. Some of the key libraries available for the developer are:

- **android.app** – gives the developer access to the app model and is the firm foundation of all applications developed for Android

- **android.content** – Makes the processes of accessing content, publishing and sending messages between apps and their components much easier

- **android.database** – Accesses data that is published by content providers. This is where you will find the SQLite management classes.

- **android.opengl** – Java interface for the OpenGL ES 3D graphics API

- **android.os** – Allows access to Provide applications along with access to operating system services like Messages, inter-process communication and system services

- **android.text** – allows text to be rendered and then manipulated on the display of the device

- **android.view** – The building blocks needed for user interfaces in an application

- **android.widget** – A collection of components for the user interface, already built, such as buttons, list views, radio buttons, layout managers an much more

- **android.webkit** – A collection of classes that are used to allow you to build the capability for web browsing into your application

Android Runtime

The next section contains one of the key components, called Dalvik Virtual Machine. This is a version of the Java Virtual Machine that has been designed specifically for Android. The Dalvik VM uses many of the core Linux features, like multi-threading and memory management, both of which are built in to the Java language. It VM allows all Android apps to run their own processes with their own version of the Dalvik virtual machine.

Android Runtime also has a number of core libraries, which are used to let app developers write their applications using Java language.

Application Framework

This layer of components includes a lot of high-level services, all of which are in the format of Java classes and all of which a developer can use in their app. The following key services are included:

- **Activity Manager** – Controls every aspect of the life cycle of the app and the activity stack

- **Content Providers** – The part that allows apps to both publish and share data with another application

- **Resource Manager** – Allows access to embedded resources that are not coded, like color settings, strings and interface layouts.

- **Notifications Manager** – Lets an app display notifications to the app user

- **View System** – A set of views that are used in the creation of the user interfaces in an app

Applications

The top layer of Android is where all the applications are and this is where your application will be installed – it can only be written to be installed in this layer.

The components of an application are the building blocks aht go to make it up. These are coupled very loosely by *AndroidManifest.xml*, which is an application manifest file that describe every part or block in the application and its interaction.

There are four main components that you can use when building your application:

- **Activities** – these say what the user interface will be and handle how the user will interact with it on their display

- **Services** – These are there to handle any of the background processes that are associated with your application

- **Broadcast Receivers** - These will handle all the communication between the applications and the operating system

- **Content Provider** - These will handle any management issues that arise with data and database management

Activities

An activity is used to present a screen that has a user interface on it, for actions to be performed by the user on their display screen. An example of this would be an email application. It could have an activity that lists all new emails while another activity would be used to compose an email and yet another for reading an email. If your application has more than a single activity, one of those activities must be earmarked as the one that is shown when the application is opened.

Activities are implemented as subclasses of the Activity class, as this example shows:

- public class MainActivity extends Activity {

- }

Services

Services are components that perform long-running operations in the background. An example of this would be a service that plays music while the user is on a different application. Or it could be fetching data via the network without stopping the user from doing something else.

Services are implemented as subclasses of the Service class, as this example shows:

- public class MyService extends Service {

- }

Broadcast Receivers

These are components that respond to messages broadcast from other applications or from the system itself. An example of this would an application that broadcasts to let another application know that new data has been downloaded and is ready for them to make use of. The receiver that intercepts the broadcast can take the appropriate action needed to make use of the data.

Broadcast receivers are implemented as subclasses of the

BroadcastReceiver class and each separate message will be broadcasted as an Intent object:

- public class MyReceiver extends BroadcastReceiver {

- public void onReceive(context,intent){}

- }

Content Providers

This component takes data from one application and gives it to other applications when requested to do so. These requests are handled by methods that are contained in the ContentReceiver class. Each must implement a set of standard APIs that allow applications to carry out transactions.

- public class MyContentProvider extends ContentProvider {

- public void onCreate(){}

- }

You will begin to understand this more when you start to build your own app.

Additional Components

There are other components that can be used in building those components, in their logic and in the way that they are attached together so that they work properly. Those additional components are:

- **Fragments** – Representative of a part of the user interface in an Activity

- **Views** – Elements of the user interface that are shown on the screen, such as list forms and buttons

- **Intents** – Messages that connect two or more components together

- **Resources** – Elements that are external, such as constants, strings and drawable pictures

- **Manifest -** A configuration file for your application

Before we move on to the next chapter, where we start to actually write your first program, do make sure that your environment is set up properly. Once that's been done, we can move on to write a simple Android application, one that you have all heard of, called "Hello, World!"

Chapter 3 – Creating Your First Android Application

When you start to create your first application for Android, you should use Eclipse IDE. Open Eclipse, select File>New>Project and then click on the wizard for Android New Application from the list of wizards that are shown. Give your application a name, for the purposes of this, we will stick with HelloWorld. Follow all the other instructions on the screen, making sure that all the other entries are set as Default right through to the last step. That will give you a project screen showing your successfully created project.

Before you even think about running your app, you need to be aware of some of the files and directories in your Android project so let's have a look at how an application is made up.

src	Contains .java source files that are needed for your project. A MainActivity.java file is included by default, and that contains an activity class that will run as soon as your app is launched on a device from the app icon
gen	Contains a computer generated .R file that is for referencing the resources contained in your project. This is one file that you must never modify
bin	Contain package files with the extension .apk. These are built during the build process. This folder also has everything else that is requires to run your Android application
res/drawable-hdpi	A directory for drawable objects that have been specifically designed for high density displays
res/layout	A directory for the files that will be used to define the user interface of your app

res/values	A directory that contains various other XML files which, in turn, hold a number of resources like color definitions and strings
AndroidManifest.xml	The manifest file responsible for the description of the characteristics of your application and for defining the individual components

In this next section, we are going to look at some of the more important application files, along with examples.

The Main Activity File

MainActivity.java is the name of the main activity code. This is in the form of an application file that will be converted into a Dalvik VM executable file and is what runs the application. The following is the default code that will have been generated for the "Hello, World!" application in the wizard you used earlier:

- package com.example.helloworld;

- import android.os.Bundle;

- import android.app.Activity;

- import android.view.Menu;

- import android.view.MenuItem;

- import android.support.v4.app.NavUtils;

- public class MainActivity extends Activity {

- @Override

- public void onCreate(Bundle savedInstanceState) {

- super.onCreate(savedInstanceState);

- setContentView(R.layout.activity_main);

- }

- @Override

- public boolean onCreateOptionsMenu(Menu menu) {

- getMenuInflater().inflate(R.menu.activity_main, menu);

- return true;

- }

- }

In this code, notice that **R.layout.activity_main** is referring to the **activity_main.xml** file that is found inside the **res/layout** folder. The method **onCreate()** is one of a large number that are configured whenever an activity loads.

The Manifest File

No matter what components you are developing within your application, you have got to declare every single component in a **manifest.xml** file. This file lives at the root of the project directory for the application and is an interface between the application and the operating system. If your component is not declared in that file, the operating system will not consider it. An example of a default manifest file is:

- <manifest xmlns:android="http://schemas.android.com/apk/res/android"

- package="com.example.helloworld"

- android:versionCode="1"

- android:versionName="1.0" >

- <uses-sdk

- android:minSdkVersion="8"

- android:targetSdkVersion="22" />

- <application

- android:icon="@drawable/ic_launcher"

- android:label="@string/app_name"

- android:theme="@style/AppTheme" >

- <activity

- android:name=".MainActivity"

- android:label="@string/title_activity_main" >

- <intent-filter>

- <action android:name="android.intent.action.MAIN" />

- <category android:name="android.intent.category.LAUNCHER "/>

- </intent-filter>

- </activity>

- </application>

- </manifest>

The <application>...</application> tags contain the components that relate to your application. The attribute named **android:icon** points to the icon for the application that is found under **res/drawable-hdpi.** The application in the example is using an image that I called **ic_launcher.png**, which is in the drawable folders.

The <activity> tag specifies an activity and the attribute **android:name** is used to specify the class name of the Activity subclass. The class name is fully qualified. The **android:label** attributes are used to specify a certain string that is to be used to label the activity. Using the <activity> tags, you can specify as many activities as you want.

Android.intent.action.MAIN is the name of the action used in the intent filter. The name indicates that the activity is the starting point for your application. **Android.intent.category.LAUNCHER** is the name of the intent filter category and it is used to indicate that a launcher icon on a device can be used to open the application

@string is referring to the **strings.xml** file that I will talk more about in a bit. **@string/app** is referring to the string called **app_name** that is defined within the strings.xml file. In this case, it is "Hello, World!" but many other strings can be populated in the application as well.

Below is a list of the tag that can be used in the manifest file as a way of specifying certain components in the Android application:

- <activity>elements for activities

- <service> elements for services

- <receiver> elements for broadcast receivers

- <provider> elements for content providers

The Strings File

The file named **strings.xml** can be found inside the **res/values** folder. It is here that all the text used in your application is stored. An example of this would the names that you put on buttons or labels, default text and any other similar string type. An example of what a default strings file would look like is:

- <resources>

- <string name="app_name">HelloWorld</string>

- <string name="hello_world">Hello world!</string>

- <string name="menu_settings">Settings</string>

- <string name="title_activity_main">MainActivity</string>

- </resources>

The R File

It is the **gen/com.example.helloworld/R.java** file that holds the activity Java files and the resource files, like strings.xml, together. The file is generate automatically and must not be modified. An example of what an R.java file would look like is:

- /* AUTO-GENERATED FILE. DO NOT MODIFY.

- *

- This class was automatically generated by the

- aapt tool from the resource data it found. It

- should not be modified by hand.

- */

- package com.example.helloworld;

- public final class R {

- public static final class attr {

- }

- public static final class dimen {

- public static final int padding_large=0x7f040002;

- public static final int padding_medium=0x7f040001;

- public static final int padding_small=0x7f040000;

- }

- public static final class drawable {

- public static final int ic_action_search=0x7f020000;

- public static final int ic_launcher=0x7f020001;

- }

- public static final class id {

- public static final int menu_settings=0x7f080000;

- }

- public static final class layout {

- public static final int activity_main=0x7f030000;

- }

- public static final class menu {

- public static final int activity_main=0x7f070000;

- }

- public static final class string {

- public static final int app_name=0x7f050000;

- public static final int hello_world=0x7f050001;

- public static final int menu_settings=0x7f050002;

- public static final int
  title_activity_main=0x7f050003;

- }

- public static final class style {

- public static final int AppTheme=0x7f060000;

- }

- }

The Layout File

In the **res/layout** directory you will find he layout file called **activity_main.xml.** This is the file that your application references when building the interface; be prepared to make numerous modifications to this file as you change the layout of the application. For the "Hello, World!" application, the file will contain the following default layout content:

- <RelativeLayout
  xmlns:android="http://schemas.android.com/apk/re
  s/android"

- xmlns:tools="http://schemas.android.com/tools"

- android:layout_width="match_parent"

- android:layout_height="match_parent" >

- <TextView

- android:layout_width="wrap_content"

- android:layout_height="wrap_content"

- android:layout_centerHorizontal="true"

- android:layout_centerVertical="true"

- android:padding="@dimen/padding_medium"

- android:text="@string/hello_world"

- tools:context=".MainActivity" />

- </RelativeLayout>

TextView is an Android control that is used in building the GUI. It will contain a number of different attributes, such as **android:layout_height, android:layout_width,** etc. These are all used to control different aspects of the application layout, such as height and width. **@string** is referring to the strings.xml file, which can be found in the res/values folder. In the case of this example, **@string/hello_world** is referring to the hello string that is defined in the strings.xml file.

Running the Application

Ok, now it's time to try and run that "Hello, World!" application you created. Open up Eclipse, open a project activity file and click on the Run icon in the toolbar. When you set up your environment part of it would have been to create an AVD so Eclipse will install your app to the AVD and start it. If all is well, you will see an emulator window that prints your text, "Hello, World!"

Congratulations, you have created your very first Android application. The rest of this chapter is designed to help you become an even better developer. To be fair, what you have used so far is very little in terms of what you can use to build a decent android application. Quite aside from the coding, you need to look at other resources, such as the static content used by your code, i.e. bitmaps, layout definitions, colors, animation instructions, user interface strings and much more besides. All of these resources will be maintained inside separate sub directories, all fond under the project directory called **res/.**

Next, we are going to talk about organizing the resources you have used in your application, some alternatives that you can look at and how to access them in the applications.

How to Organize the Resources in Eclipse

Each separate resource should be in a specific sub directory of the res/ directory. An example of the hierarchy for a simple project would look something like this:

- MyProject/

- src/

- MyActivity.java

- res/

- drawable/

- icon.png

- layout/

- activity_main.xml

- info.xml

- values/

- strings.xml

Inside the following example directory, we have subdirectories for image resources, string resources and tow layout resources.

- MyProject/

- src/

  o main/

  o java/

  o MyActivity.java

- res/

- drawable/

- icon.png

- layout/

- activity_main.xml

- info.xml

- values/

- strings.xml

The next table shows you how the resource directories are supported inside the res/ project directory:

Directory	Resource Type
anim/	These are XML files that define animations of properties. They are saved to a folder called res/anim/ and can be accessed via the R.anim class
color/	These are XML files that define state lists of colors. They are saved in a folder called res/color and are accessed via the R.color class
drawable/	These are image files like XML, .jpg, .png or .gif that are compiled into shapes, state lists, bitmaps, animation drawables etc. They are saved to a folder called res/drawable and can be accessed via the R/drawable class
layout/	These are XML files that are used to define the layout of a user interface. They are saved to a folder called res/layout and can be accessed via the R.layout class
menu/	These are XML files that are used to define menus in the applications, such as a Sub menu, Context menu or an Options menu. They are saved to a folder called res/menu and can be accessed via the R. menu class
raw/	These are arbitrary files that are saved in their raw form and to open the you must call **Resources.openRawResources()** using the

	resource ID of **R.raw.filename**
values/	These are XML files that have simple values in them, such as integers, string and colors. Some of the conventions for naming the resources that can be created in this directory are: • arrays.xml – for resource arrays, found in the class called R.array • integers.xml – for resource integers, found in the class called R.integer • bools.xml – for resource booleans, found in the class called R.bool • colors.xml – for resource colors, found in the class called R.color • dimens.xml – for dimension values and found in the class called R.dimen • strings.xml – for string values and found in the class called R.string • styles.xml – for styles and fond in the class called R.style
xml/	These are arbitrary XML files that can be called with **Resources.getXML()** to be read at runtime

Chapter 4 – Alternative Resources

When you write your application, it should have alternative resources that support certain device configurations. For example, there should be alternative drawable resources, like images, for devices that have different screen resolutions. There should be alternative string resources to support different languages. At runtime, the operating system will detect what the configuration of the device is and will load in the right resources for the application.

To specify alternatives that are specific to configuration for a resource set, you should follow these steps:

- First, in **res/** you should create a new directory with the name in this format - **<resources_name>-<config_qualifier>**. In this case, **resources_name** can be any of the resources that we talked about in the last chapter – see the table at the end of the chapter. The qualifier is to specify a single configuration that the resources are going to be used for.

- Second, you should save the alternative resources into the directory you have just created. The files must be names the same as the default resource files that are shown in the following example although the content of each file will be specific to the alternative resource.

This example shows images that are specified for a default screen resolution, coupled with alternatives for a high-resolution screen:

- MyProject/

- src/

- main/

- java/

- MyActivity.java

- res/

- drawable/

- icon.png

- background.png

- drawable-hdpi/

- icon.png

- background.png

- layout/

- activity_main.xml

- info.xml

- values/

- strings.xml

Here is a further example that shows the layout for default languages and then an alternative for the Arabic language:

- MyProject/

- src/

  o main/

  o java/

  o MyActivity.java

- res/

- drawable/

- icon.png

- background.png

- drawable-hdpi/

- icon.png

- background.png

- layout/

- activity_main.xml

- info.xml

- layout-ar/

- main.xml

- values/

- strings.xml

Accessing Resources

When you are developing your app, you will have to access resources that are defined, be they in your code or located in the layout XML files. This next section shows you how to access the resources either way.

Accessing Resources in Code

When you compile your Android application R class is automatically generated. This contains all the resource IDs for all the resources that are in your res/ directory. The R class can be used to access the specific resource using the specific sub directory and the resource.

For example, if you want to access the **res/drawable/myimage.png** and then set an **ImageView**, you would use this code:

- ImageView imageView = (ImageView) findViewById(R.id.myimageview);

- imageView.setImageResource(R.drawable.myimage);

The first line of this code uses **R.id.myimageview** to get the **ImageView** that has been defined with the id **myimageview** and is in a layout file. The second line uses **R.drawable.myimage** to get an image that is called **myimage** from the drawable sub directory in the /res directory.

Another example shows **res/values/strings.xml** with this definition:

- <?xml version="1.0" encoding="utf-8"?>

- <resources>

- <string name="hello">Hello, World!</string>

- </resources>

You can now set the text for a **TextView** object that has the ID **msg** by using a resource ID as such:

- TextView msgTextView = (TextView) findViewById(R.id.msg);

- msgTextView.setText(R.string.hello);

The next example shows a layout **res/layout/activity_main.xml** with this definition:

- <?xml version="1.0" encoding="utf-8"?>

- <LinearLayout xmlns:android="http://schemas.android.com/apk/res/android"

- android:layout_width="fill_parent"

- android:layout_height="fill_parent"

- android:orientation="vertical" >

- <TextView android:id="@+id/text"

- android:layout_width="wrap_content"

- android:layout_height="wrap_content"

- android:text="Hello, I am a TextView" />

- <Button android:id="@+id/button"

- android:layout_width="wrap_content"

- android:layout_height="wrap_content"

- android:text="Hello, I am a Button" />

- </LinearLayout>

The code will load the layout for an Activity as follows in the **onCreate()** method:

- public void onCreate(Bundle savedInstanceState) {

- super.onCreate(savedInstanceState);

- setContentView(R.layout.main_activity);

- }

Accessing Resources in XML

Look at this resource xml file **res/values/strings.xml** and note that it has a color and a string resource in it:

- `<?xml version="1.0" encoding="utf-8"?>`

- `<resources>`

- `<color name="opaque_red">#f00</color>`

- `<string name="hello">Hello!</string>`

- `</resources>`

You can now use these resources in the layout file below to set the text string and text color like this:

- `<?xml version="1.0" encoding="utf-8"?>`

- `<EditText xmlns:android="http://schemas.android.com/apk/res/android"`

- `android:layout_width="fill_parent"`

- `android:layout_height="fill_parent"`

- `android:textColor="@color/opaque_red"`

- `android:text="@string/hello" />`

Now go back through the chapter where we created the "Hello, World!" example and you should now have a much better understanding of all the concepts that have been used.

Next we are going to delve a little deeper into the world of Android programming and look at more elements that make up an application.

All code in the following chapters is fully attributed to <u>www.tutorialspoint.com</u>

Chapter 5 – Activity

In Android programming, an activity is a representation of one screen that contains a user interface. It is similar to the frame or window that you might see in Java programming. Activity is a subclass of the ContextThemeWrapper class.

If you are familiar with Java or C/C++ languages then you will already have spotted what your Android program begins with – the **main()** function. In much the same way as most other computer programming languages, the Android program is initiated using an activity that begins with by calling the **onCreate()** method.

The Activity class is responsible for defining call back, such as events. There is no need to implement every callback method but you do need to have an understanding of what each one does and how to implement it to make sure that your app is working the way it should do.

Callback	Description
onCreate()	The first callback, called at the time the activity is initially created
onStart()	Called when an activity is seen by the user
onResume()	Called when the app user begins interaction with the app
onPause()	An activity that has been paused cannot get any input from the user nor can it execute code. It is called when the activity in use is paused and the activity before is resumed.
onStop()	Called when an activity can no longer be seen
onDestroy()	Called before the system destroys an activity
onRestart()	Called when an activity is restarted after being stopped

An Example

The following example will show you the steps that you need to understand about the life cycle of an Android app activity. You can use these stops to make some modifications to the HelloWorld example we used earlier:

Step	Description
1	Use Eclipse IDE and create an app called HelloWorld. Use package com.example.helloworld
2	Modify MainActivity.java (see below) but leave all other files as they are
3	Run the app to open the emulator and see what the result is of the modifications

The following code is the content of **src/com.example.helloworld/MainActivity.java** after the modification. All of the basic required life cycle method are included and we have used **Log.d()** to throw the log messages up:

- package com.example.helloworld;

- import android.os.Bundle;

- import android.app.Activity;

- import android.util.Log;

- public class MainActivity extends Activity {

- String msg = "Android : ";

- /** Called when the activity is first created. */

- @Override

- public void onCreate(Bundle savedInstanceState) {

- super.onCreate(savedInstanceState);

- setContentView(R.layout.activity_main);

- Log.d(msg, "The onCreate() event");

- }

- /** Called when the activity is about to become visible. */

- @Override

- protected void onStart() {

- super.onStart();

- Log.d(msg, "The onStart() event");

- }

- /** Called when the activity has become visible. */

- @Override

- protected void onResume() {

- super.onResume();

- Log.d(msg, "The onResume() event");

- }

- /** Called when another activity is taking focus. */

- @Override

- protected void onPause() {

- super.onPause();

- Log.d(msg, "The onPause() event");

- }

- /** Called when the activity is no longer visible. */

- @Override

- protected void onStop() {

- super.onStop();

- Log.d(msg, "The onStop() event");

- }

- /** Called just before the activity is destroyed. */

- @Override

- public void onDestroy() {

- super.onDestroy();

- Log.d(msg, "The onDestroy() event");

- }

- }

Activity classes load the UI components by using the XML file that is found in **res/layout** – a folder in your project. The next statement is used to load the UI components that are in **res/layout/activity_main.xml:**

- setContentView(R.layout.activity_main);

Applications are able to have more than one activity without any restrictions. Each activity that is defined for the app has to be declared in **AndroidManifest.xml** and the main activity has to be declared with an <intent-filter>. This filter includes the LAUNCHER category and the MAIN action, as you can see in the following code:

- <manifest xmlns:android="http://schemas.android.com/apk/res/android"

- package="com.example.helloworld"

- android:versionCode="1"

- android:versionName="1.0" >

- <uses-sdk

- android:minSdkVersion="8"

- android:targetSdkVersion="22" />

- <application

- android:icon="@drawable/ic_launcher"

- android:label="@string/app_name"

- android:theme="@style/AppTheme" >

- ```
  <activity
  ```
- ```
  android:name=".MainActivity"
  ```
- ```
  android:label="@string/title_activity_main" >
  ```

- ```
  <intent-filter>
  ```
- ```
  <action android:name="android.intent.action.MAIN"
  />
  ```
- ```
  <category
  android:name="android.intent.category.LAUNCHER
  "/>
  ```
- ```
  </intent-filter>
  ```

- ```
  </activity>
  ```

- ```
  </application>
  ```
- ```
  </manifest>
  ```

If you do not declare either LAUNCHER or MAIN for an activity, the ion for the application will not show up in the list of apps on the home screen.

Let's have a go at running your newly modified Hello World! app. I am going to assume that you have followed this book all the way so far and have already created your AVD when you set up your environment. To run the new app, open up a project activity file in Eclipse and click on the Run icon in the toolbar. The app will then be installed, by Eclipse, into your AVD and it will be started up. If all is OK, you will see the emulator window and the following messages should show up in the LogCat window that is in Eclipse:

- 07-19 15:00:43.405: D/Android :(866): The onCreate() event

- 07-19 15:00:43.405: D/Android :(866): The onStart() event

- 07-19 15:00:43.415: D/Android :(866): The onResume() event

Now click on the Red button that you see on the Android emulator – it looks like a telephone receiver. The following will then be generated in the LogCat window:

- 07-19 15:01:10.995: D/Android :(866): The onPause() event

- 07-19 15:01:12.705: D/Android :(866): The onStop() event

Now click the Menu button on the emulator and the following will appear in the LogCat window:

- 07-19 15:01:13.995: D/Android :(866): The onStart() event

- 07-19 15:01:14.705: D/Android :(866): The onResume() event

Finally, click on the Back on the emulator and the following messages will be generated.

- 07-19 15:33:15.687: D/Android :(992): The onPause() event

- 07-19 15:33:15.525: D/Android :(992): The onStop() event

- 07-19 15:33:15.525: D/Android :(992): The onDestroy() event

That completes an Activity Life Cycle for any Android app.

Chapter 6 – Services

Services are back road components, performing operations that are long running without having to interact with an app user. A service will work even when the application has been destroyed and it can be in two states:

- **Started** – the service is started when a component, such as an activity, of the application begins by calling the startService(). Once the service has started it will run in the background for as long as needed even when the starting component has been destroyed

- **Bound** - The service is bound when a component call bindService(). This offers an interface that lets a components interact with the service, to send out requests, return results and does so across processes with IPC – interprocess communication

Services also have life-cycle callback methods that can be implemented as a way of monitoring any change in the state of the service, allowing the developer to work where it is needed.

In order to create a service, you first need to make a Java class that will extend the base class or a subclass of the service. The base class defines a number of different callback methods, the more important of which are in the following table. While you do not need to implement all of these, you must understand them and now which ones to implement so your app works as it should.

Callback	Description
onStartCommand()	Called when a component calls startService(), requesting that the service be started. If this method is implemented, it is down to you to stop it when required by using stopService() or stopSelf()
onBind()	Called when bindService () is called by a component. If this method s implemented it is down to you to give the user an interface to use for communication with the

	service. You do this by returning IBinder. This must always be implements but you can return **null** if you are not allowing binding
onUnBind()	Called when every user has disconnected from the published interface
onReBind()	Called when a new user connects, after the system has been told that all users have disconnected
onCreate()	Called when the onStartCommand() is used to initially create the serve. This can also be started with the onBind() method and is required for a one-time-only setup
onDestroy()	Called when the service is no longer in use and is set to be destroyed. The system should automatically implement this as a way of cleaning up resources

An Example

The following code is a "skeleton service" that shows you each life-cycle method:

- package com.tutorialspoint;

- import android.app.Service;

- import android.os.IBinder;

- import android.content.Intent;

- import android.os.Bundle;

- public class HelloService extends Service {

- /** indicates how to behave if the service is killed */

- int mStartMode;

- /** interface for clients that bind */

- IBinder mBinder;

- /** indicates whether onRebind should be used */

- boolean mAllowRebind;

- /** Called when the service is being created. */

- @Override

- public void onCreate() {

- }

- /** The service is starting, due to a call to startService() */

- @Override

- public int onStartCommand(Intent intent, int flags, int startId) {

- return mStartMode;

- }

- /** A client is binding to the service with bindService() */

- @Override

- public IBinder onBind(Intent intent) {

- return mBinder;

- }

- /** Called when all clients have unbound with unbindService() */

- @Override

- public boolean onUnbind(Intent intent) {

- return mAllowRebind;

- }

- /** Called when a client is binding to the service with bindService()*/

- @Override

- public void onRebind(Intent intent) {

- }

- /** Called when The service is no longer used and is being destroyed */

- @Override

- public void onDestroy() {

- }

- }

Another Example

This example will walk you through the steps needed to create a service. Use these steps to modify your Hello World! Application:

Step	Description
1	Use Android Studio IDE to create My Application, using the package called com.example.MyApplication
2	Modify **MainActivity.java**, adding in two methods – startService() and stopService()

3	Make a new java file called MyService.java. This is done in com.example.My Application. This new file is going to have an implementation of some service related methods
4	Use <service.../> tag in AndroidManifest.xml to define the service. Your app can more than one service with no restrictions.
5	Go into res/layout/activity_main.xml and modify it to include a pair of buttons that are in linear layout
6	Do not make any changes to any of the constants inside res/values/strings.xml as Android will take of this
7	Run the application so that the emulator starts. Check the results of the changes that you made

The following code is the modified contents of src/com.example.My Application/MainActivity.java. You can include this file in all of the basic life cycle methods and, as you will see, we have put in methods to stop and start the service – startService() and stopService().

- package com.example.My Application;

- import android.os.Bundle;

- import android.app.Activity;

- import android.view.Menu;

- import android.content.Intent;

- import android.view.View;

- public class MainActivity extends Activity {

- @Override

- public void onCreate(Bundle savedInstanceState) {

- super.onCreate(savedInstanceState);

- setContentView(R.layout.activity_main);

- }

- @Override

- public boolean onCreateOptionsMenu(Menu menu) {

- getMenuInflater().inflate(R.menu.activity_main, menu);

- return true;

- }

- // Method to start the service

- public void startService(View view) {

- startService(new Intent(getBaseContext(), MyService.class));

- }

- // Method to stop the service

- public void stopService(View view) {

- stopService(new Intent(getBaseContext(), MyService.class));

- }

- }

This code is the modified content of src/com.example.My Application/MyService.java. This file is able to contain more than one method that is associated with the service, based on the requirements of the service. We are implementing just two – onStartCommand() and onDestroy().

- package com.example.My Application;

- import android.app.Service;

- import android.content.Intent;

- import android.os.IBinder;

- import android.widget.Toast;

- public class MyService extends Service {

- @Override

- public IBinder onBind(Intent argo) {

- return null;

- }

- @Override

- public int onStartCommand(Intent intent, int flags, int startId) {

- // Let it continue running until it is stopped.

- Toast.makeText(this, "Service Started", Toast.LENGTH_LONG).show();

- return START_STICKY;

- }

- @Override

- public void onDestroy() {

- super.onDestroy();

- Toast.makeText(this, "Service Destroyed", Toast.LENGTH_LONG).show();

- }

- }

This code is the modification we made to AndroidManifest.xml. We have used the tag <service.../> to ensure the service is included:

- <manifest xmlns:android="http://schemas.android.com/apk/res/android"

- package="com.example.MyApplication"

- android:versionCode="1"

- android:versionName="1.0" >

- <uses-sdk

- android:minSdkVersion="13"

- android:targetSdkVersion="22" />

- <application

- android:icon="@drawable/ic_launcher"

- android:label="@string/app_name"

- android:theme="@style/AppTheme" >

- <activity

- android:name=".MainActivity"

- android:label="@string/title_activity_main" >

- <intent-filter>

- <action android:name="android.intent.action.MAIN" />

- <category android:name="android.intent.category.LAUNCHER "/>

- </intent-filter>

- </activity>

- <service android:name=".MyService" />

- </application>

- </manifest>

This code is the modified content of res/layout/activity_main.xml that now has two buttons:

- <RelativeLayout xmlns:android="http://schemas.android.com/apk/res/android"

- xmlns:tools="http://schemas.android.com/tools" android:layout_width="match_parent"

- android:layout_height="match_parent" android:paddingLeft="@dimen/activity_horizontal_margin"

- android:paddingRight="@dimen/activity_horizontal_margin"

- android:paddingTop="@dimen/activity_vertical_margin"

- android:paddingBottom="@dimen/activity_vertical_margin" tools:context=".MainActivity">

- <TextView

- android:id="@+id/textView1"

- android:layout_width="wrap_content"

- android:layout_height="wrap_content"

- android:text="Example of services"

- android:layout_alignParentTop="true"

- android:layout_centerHorizontal="true"

- android:textSize="30dp" />

- <TextView

- android:id="@+id/textView2"

- android:layout_width="wrap_content"

- android:layout_height="wrap_content"

- android:text="Tutorials point "

- android:textColor="#ff87ff09"

- android:textSize="30dp"

- android:layout_above="@+id/imageButton"

- android:layout_centerHorizontal="true"

- android:layout_marginBottom="40dp" />

- <ImageButton

- android:layout_width="wrap_content"

- android:layout_height="wrap_content"

- android:id="@+id/imageButton"

- android:src="@drawable/abc"

- android:layout_centerVertical="true"

- android:layout_centerHorizontal="true" />

- <Button

- android:layout_width="wrap_content"

- android:layout_height="wrap_content"

- android:id="@+id/button2"

- android:text="Start Services"

- android:onClick="startService"

- android:layout_below="@+id/imageButton"

- android:layout_centerHorizontal="true" />

- <Button

- android:layout_width="wrap_content"

- android:layout_height="wrap_content"

- android:text="Stop Services"

- android:id="@+id/button"

- android:onClick="stopService"

- android:layout_below="@+id/button2"

- android:layout_alignLeft="@+id/button2"

- android:layout_alignStart="@+id/button2"

- android:layout_alignRight="@+id/button2"

- android:layout_alignEnd="@+id/button2" />

- </RelativeLayout>

Finally, this code is the content of res/values/strings.xml that is defining two constants

- <resources>

- <string name="app_name">My Application</string>

- <string name="menu_settings">Settings</string>

- <string name="title_activity_main">MainActivity</string>

- </resources>

Have a go at running the modified version of Hello World! Again, I will assume that you have your AVD created so open a project activity file from Android Studio and click on Run in the toolbar. The app will now be installed into the AVD and it will be started. If it is all OK, you will see the emulator window.

Click on the button that says Start Service and your service will begin. You should see a message at the bottom of the emulator saying "Service Started".

Click on Stop Service to stop it.

Chapter 7 – Broadcast Receivers

A broadcast receiver is used to broadcast a message that comes from the system or from another application. The message is sometimes known as an intent or an event. An example of this is an application that sends a message to tell other applications that data has been or is ready to download into the device and is there for use. The broadcast receiver will intercept the message and take the action needed.

The following are the two vital steps to making BroadcastReceiver work for intents broadcast by the system:

- Create the Broadcast Receiver

- Register the Broadcast Receiver

If you intend to implement custom intents, there is an extra step you need to do – create and then broadcast the intents.

Creating a Broadcast Receiver

The receiver is a subclass of BroadcastReceiver and it will override the onReceive() method, which is where the message are received as parameters for an intent object

- public class MyReceiver extends BroadcastReceiver {

- @Override

- public void onReceive(Context context, Intent intent) {

- Toast.makeText(context, "Intent Detected.", Toast.LENGTH_LONG).show();

- }

- }

Registering a Receiver

Applications listen out for certain intents by registering the receiver n AndroidManifet.xml. For this, we will register MyReceiver for ACTION_BOOT_COMPLETED, which is an event generated by the system. Once the system has finished the boot process, the Android will fire the event.

- <application

- android:icon="@drawable/ic_launcher"

- android:label="@string/app_name"

- android:theme="@style/AppTheme" >

- <receiver android:name="MyReceiver">

- <intent-filter>

- <action
  android:name="android.intent.action.BOOT_COMPL
  ETED">

- </action>

- </intent-filter>

- </receiver>

- </application>

Because of this, when you reboot your Android device, BroadcastReceiver will intercept it and the logic that is in onReceive() is implemented

There are a number of events that are generated by the system that are defined as static fields in Intent. These are the more important events:

Constant	Description
android.intent.action.BATTERY_CHANGED	Broadcast that says what the charging state of the device is, including battery level and any other information pertaining to the battery and/or charge
android.intent.action.BATTERY_LOW	Indication of a low battery on a device
android.intent.action.BATTERY_OKAY	Indication that the battery level is OK, following a low charge level
android.intent.action.BOOT_COMPLETED	Broadcast as soon as the system boot has finished
android.intent.action.BUG_REPORT	Shows bug reporting activity
android.intent.action.CALL	Sends out a call to a data-specified person
android.intent.action.CALL_BUTTON	Broadcast when a user hits the "call" button to access the dialer app or any other UI that is appropriate to making a phone call
android.intent.action.DATE_CHANGED	Broadcasts a message to say that the date has changed

android.intent.action.REBOOT	Tells the device it needs to reboot

Broadcasting a Custom Intent

If you app is going to generate custom intents and send them, you will need to actually create the intents and send them with the sendBroadcast() method, by putting it in the activity class. The sendStickyBroadcast(Intent) method will make the Intent hang around after the broadcast is finished.

- public void broadcastIntent(View view)

- {

- Intent = new Intent();

- intent.setAction("com.tutorialspoint.CUSTOM_INTENT");

- sendBroadcast(intent);

- }

The com.tutorialspoint.CUSTOM_INTENT may be registered in the same way that the system-generated intent was registered.

- <application

- android:icon="@drawable/ic_launcher"

- android:label="@string/app_name"

- android:theme="@style/AppTheme" >

- <receiver android:name="MyReceiver">

- <intent-filter>

- <action android:name="com.tutorialspoint.CUSTOM_INTENT">

- </action>

- </intent-filter>

- </receiver>

- </application>

Example

The following will tell you how to intercept a custom intent by creating the BroadcastReceiver. When you have familiarized yourself with custom intents, you can go ahead and modify your application so that it can intercept intents that are generated by the system. Use these steps to modify your Hello World! Application:

Step	Description
1	Using Android Studio, create an application and give it the name asMy Application. This should go into a package called com.example.My Application
2	Make a modification to MainActivity.java and add in a broadcastIntent() method
3	In the package called com.example.My Application, make a new java file and call it MyReceiver.java. This will define BroadcastReceiver.
4	Applications are able to take more than system and custom intent with no restrictions. Each of the intents that are to be intercepted have to be registered in AndroidManifest.xml and you do this with a <receiver...> tag
5	The default content of res/layout/activity_mai.xml needs to be modified next to add in a broadcast intent button

6	Do not modify the string file values as Android will do this itself
7	Run your application so that the emulator opens and check the results of your modifications

The following code is the modified content of src/com.example.My Application/MainActivity.java. Note that we modified it to contain broadcastIntent() so that we can broadcast custom intents:

- package com.example.My Application;

- import android.os.Bundle;

- import android.app.Activity;

- import android.view.Menu;

- import android.content.Intent;

- import android.view.View;

- public class MainActivity extends Activity {

- @Override

- public void onCreate(Bundle savedInstanceState) {

- super.onCreate(savedInstanceState);

- setContentView(R.layout.activity_main);

- }

- @Override

- public boolean onCreateOptionsMenu(Menu menu) {

- getMenuInflater().inflate(R.menu.activity_main, menu);

- return true;

- }

- // broadcast a custom intent.

- public void broadcastIntent(View view){

- Intent intent = new Intent();

- intent.setAction("com.tutorialspoint.CUSTOM_INTE NT");

- sendBroadcast(intent);

- }

- }

This next code is the new content of src/com.example.My Application/MyReceiver.java:

- package com.example.My Application;

- import android.content.BroadcastReceiver;

- import android.content.Context;

- import android.content.Intent;

- import android.widget.Toast;

- public class MyReceiver extends BroadcastReceiver {

- @Override

- public void onReceive(Context context, Intent intent) {

- Toast.makeText(context, "Intent Detected.", Toast.LENGTH_LONG).show();

- }

- }

The next code is the new content of AndroidManifest.xml where we used the tag <service...> to make sure the service was included:

- <manifest xmlns:android="http://schemas.android.com/apk/res/android"

- package="com.example.My Application"

- android:versionCode="1"

- android:versionName="1.0" >

- <uses-sdk

- android:minSdkVersion="8"

- android:targetSdkVersion="22" />

- <application

- android:icon="@drawable/ic_launcher"

- android:label="@string/app_name"

- android:theme="@style/AppTheme" >

- <activity

- android:name=".MainActivity"

- android:label="@string/title_activity_main" >

- <intent-filter>

- <action android:name="android.intent.action.MAIN" />

- <category android:name="android.intent.category.LAUNCHER "/>

- </intent-filter>

- </activity>

- <receiver android:name="MyReceiver">

- <intent-filter>

- <action android:name="com.tutorialspoint.CUSTOM_INTENT">

- </action>

- </intent-filter>

- </receiver>

- </application>

- </manifest>

The next code is the res/layout/activity_main.xml file and we included a broadcast button:

- <RelativeLayout xmlns:android="http://schemas.android.com/apk/res/android"

- xmlns:tools="http://schemas.android.com/tools" android:layout_width="match_parent"

- android:layout_height="match_parent" android:paddingLeft="@dimen/activity_horizontal_ margin"

- android:paddingRight="@dimen/activity_horizontal _margin"

- android:paddingTop="@dimen/activity_vertical_mar gin"

- android:paddingBottom="@dimen/activity_vertical_ margin" tools:context=".MainActivity">

- \<TextView

- android:id="@+id/textView1"

- android:layout_width="wrap_content"

- android:layout_height="wrap_content"

- android:text="Example of Broadcast"

- android:layout_alignParentTop="true"

- android:layout_centerHorizontal="true"

- android:textSize="30dp" />

- <TextView

- android:id="@+id/textView2"

- android:layout_width="wrap_content"

- android:layout_height="wrap_content"

- android:text="Tutorials point "

- android:textColor="#ff87ff09"

- android:textSize="30dp"

- android:layout_above="@+id/imageButton"

- android:layout_centerHorizontal="true"

- android:layout_marginBottom="40dp" />

- <ImageButton

- android:layout_width="wrap_content"

- android:layout_height="wrap_content"

- android:id="@+id/imageButton"

- android:src="@drawable/abc"

- android:layout_centerVertical="true"

- android:layout_centerHorizontal="true" />

- <Button

- android:layout_width="wrap_content"

- android:layout_height="wrap_content"

- android:id="@+id/button2"

- android:text="Broadcast Intent"

- android:onClick="broadcastIntent"

- android:layout_below="@+id/imageButton"

- android:layout_centerHorizontal="true" />

- </RelativeLayout>

The final code is the res/vale/strng.ml file where we defined a couple of constants:

- <resources>

- <string name="menu_settings">Settings</string>

- <string name="title_activity_main">My
  Application</string>

- </resources>

Run the modified version of HelloWorld using Android Studio. Open up an activity file and click on Run. The app is installed to your AVD and if all is OK, the emulator will open.

To broadcast the custom intent, click the button that says Broadcast Intent. The custom intent called com.tutorialspoint.CUSTOM_INTENT should be intercepted by MyReciver, which is the BroadcastReceiver you registered. A toast should show up at the bottom of your emulator.

Chapter 8 – Content Provider

The content provider takes data from an application and gives t to another when requested to do so. The methods in the ContentResolver class will handle all of these requests. Content providers use a number of methods to store data, including file, databases and networks.

A content provider will let you put the content in one central place and allow as many applications as needed to access that content whenever they need it. The content provider acts like a database in that a developer is able to edit the content, query it, and use methods such as delete(), insert(), update() and query(). In almost every case, SQLite databases are used for data storage.'

Content providers are implemented as subclasses of the ContentProvider class and they have to implement a set of standard APIs. These API's will enable other apps to carry out transactions:

- public class My Application extends ContentProvider {

- }

- Content URIs

For a content provider to be queried, you must specify a query string. This is in the format of a URI, which will have this format:

- <prefix>://<authority>/<data_type>/<id>

Each part of the URI I described below:

- **Prefix** – always set as content://

- **Authority** - the specific content provider name, i.e. contacts.browser. If using a third party content provider, you can specify a fully qualified name, i.e. com.tutorialspoint.statusprovider

- **data_type** – specifies the data type provided by the specified provider, i.e. if you use Contactscontent as the provider, the data path is **people** and the path would be content://contacts/people

- **id** - specifies the record that is being requested, i.e. if you want record 5 from the content provider, the URI would be content://contacts/people/5

Create the Content Provider

There are a few steps that you need to go through in order to create a content provider:

1. Create the content Provider class, extending ContentProvider base class

2. Define the URI address for the content provider – this is how the data will be accessed

3. Create a database for the data to be stored in. This will be a SQLite database and the framework must override the onCreate() method, which uses the Open Helper method in SQLite to either open or create a database for the provider. When the app is launched, onCreate() is called on the app thread for each content provider

4. The next step is to implement the queries for Content Provider so that they each perform a specific operation in the database

5. Lastly, use the <provider...> tag to register the Content Provider in the activity file

The following list are the methods that must be overridden in the Content Provider class if your Content Provider is to work:

- **onCreate()** - Called at the time the Content Provider is started

- **query()** – gets the client request and returns the result as a Cursor object

- **insert()** – puts a new record into the provider

- **delete()** - deletes a record from the provider

- **update()** - updates a record from the provider

- **getType()** – determines the MIME data type of the URI and returns it

An Example

The following tells you how to make a ContentProvider:

Step	Description
1	Use Android Studio IDE to make a ContentProvider and call it My Application. This is in the package called com.example.My Application and it has a blank activity

2	Make a modification to the MainActivity.java file to provide it with new methods – onClickAddName() and onClickRetrieveStudents
3	Now make a new .java file and call it StudentsProvider.java. Again, this will be in the package called com.example.My Application and it will be used to define the provider and the methods associated with it
4	Use the tag <provider.../> to register the provider in AndroidManifest.xml
5	The default content of res/layout/activity_main.xml needs to be modified next to add in a GUI that adds the records
6	Do not make any changes to string.xml as Android will do that.
7	Lastly, run your modified application so the emulator opens and check the results of the changes

The following code is the modified content of src/com.example.My Application/MainActivity.java. Note that this contains the two new methods called onClickAddName() and onClickRetrieveStudents() to help the user to interact with the application:

- package com.example.My Application;

- import android.net.Uri;

- import android.os.Bundle;

- import android.app.Activity;

- import android.content.ContentValues;

- import android.content.CursorLoader;

- import android.database.Cursor;

- import android.view.Menu;

- import android.view.View;

- import android.widget.EditText;

- import android.widget.Toast;

- public class MainActivity extends Activity {

- @Override

- protected void onCreate(Bundle savedInstanceState) {

- super.onCreate(savedInstanceState);

- setContentView(R.layout.activity_main);

- }

- @Override

- public boolean onCreateOptionsMenu(Menu menu) {

- getMenuInflater().inflate(R.menu.main, menu);

- return true;

- }

- public void onClickAddName(View view) {

- // Add a new student record

- ContentValues values = new ContentValues();

- values.put(StudentsProvider.NAME,

- ((EditText)findViewById(R.id.editText2)).getText().to String());

- values.put(StudentsProvider.GRADE,

- ((EditText)findViewById(R.id.editText3)).getText().to String());

- Uri uri = getContentResolver().insert(

- StudentsProvider.CONTENT_URI, values);

- Toast.makeText(getBaseContext(),

- uri.toString(), Toast.LENGTH_LONG).show();

- }

- public void onClickRetrieveStudents(View view) {

- // Retrieve student records

- String URL = "content://com.example.provider.College/students";

- Uri students = Uri.parse(URL);

- Cursor c = managedQuery(students, null, null, null, "name");

- if (c.moveToFirst()) {

- do{

- Toast.makeText(this,

- c.getString(c.getColumnIndex(StudentsProvider._ID)) +

- ", " + c.getString(c.getColumnIndex(StudentsProvider.NAME)) +

- ", " + c.getString(c.getColumnIndex(StudentsProvider.GRADE)),

- Toast.LENGTH_SHORT).show();

- } while (c.moveToNext());

- }

- }

- }

Next, you can make a new file called StudentsProvider.java. This is to be done in com.example.My Applications and the finished file, src/com.example.My Application/StudentsProvider.java should be:

- package com.example.My Application;

- import java.util.HashMap;

- import android.content.ContentProvider;

- import android.content.ContentUris;

- import android.content.ContentValues;

- import android.content.Context;

- import android.content.UriMatcher;

- import android.database.Cursor;

- import android.database.SQLException;

- import android.database.sqlite.SQLiteDatabase;

- import android.database.sqlite.SQLiteOpenHelper;

- import android.database.sqlite.SQLiteQueryBuilder;

- import android.net.Uri;

- import android.text.TextUtils;

- public class StudentsProvider extends ContentProvider {

- static final String PROVIDER_NAME = "com.example.provider.College";

- static final String URL = "content://" + PROVIDER_NAME + "/students";

- static final Uri CONTENT_URI = Uri.parse(URL);

- static final String _ID = "_id";

- static final String NAME = "name";

- static final String GRADE = "grade";

- private static HashMap<String, String> STUDENTS_PROJECTION_MAP;

- static final int STUDENTS = 1;

- static final int STUDENT_ID = 2;

- static final UriMatcher uriMatcher;

- static{

- uriMatcher = new
  UriMatcher(UriMatcher.NO_MATCH);

- uriMatcher.addURI(PROVIDER_NAME, "students",
  STUDENTS);

- uriMatcher.addURI(PROVIDER_NAME,
  "students/#", STUDENT_ID);

- }

- /**

- Database specific constant declarations

- */

- private SQLiteDatabase db;

- static final String DATABASE_NAME = "College";

- static final String STUDENTS_TABLE_NAME = "students";

- static final int DATABASE_VERSION = 1;

- static final String CREATE_DB_TABLE =

- " CREATE TABLE " + STUDENTS_TABLE_NAME +

- " (_id INTEGER PRIMARY KEY AUTOINCREMENT, " +

- " name TEXT NOT NULL, " +

- " grade TEXT NOT NULL);";

- /**

- Helper class that actually creates and manages

- the provider's underlying data repository.

- */

- private static class DatabaseHelper extends SQLiteOpenHelper {

- DatabaseHelper(Context context){

- super(context, DATABASE_NAME, null, DATABASE_VERSION);

- }

- @Override

- public void onCreate(SQLiteDatabase db)

- {

- db.execSQL(CREATE_DB_TABLE);

- }

- @Override

- public void onUpgrade(SQLiteDatabase db, int oldVersion, int newVersion) {

- db.execSQL("DROP TABLE IF EXISTS " + STUDENTS_TABLE_NAME);

- onCreate(db);

- }

- }

- @Override

- public boolean onCreate() {

- Context context = getContext();

- DatabaseHelper dbHelper = new DatabaseHelper(context);

- /**

- Create a writeable database which will trigger its

- creation if it doesn't already exist.

- */

- db = dbHelper.getWritableDatabase();

- return (db == null)? false:true;

- }

- @Override

- public Uri insert(Uri uri, ContentValues values) {

- /**

- Add a new student record

- */

- long rowID = db.insert(
  STUDENTS_TABLE_NAME, "", values);

- /**

- If record is added successfully

- */

- if (rowID > 0)

- {

- Uri _uri =
  ContentUris.withAppendedId(CONTENT_URI,
  rowID);

- getContext().getContentResolver().notifyChange(_uri,
  null);

- return _uri;

- }

- throw new SQLException("Failed to add a record into
  " + uri);

- }

- @Override

- public Cursor query(Uri uri, String[] projection, String selection,String[] selectionArgs, String sortOrder) {

- SQLiteQueryBuilder qb = new SQLiteQueryBuilder();

- qb.setTables(STUDENTS_TABLE_NAME);

- switch (uriMatcher.match(uri)) {

- case STUDENTS:

- qb.setProjectionMap(STUDENTS_PROJECTION_M AP);

- break;

- case STUDENT_ID:

- qb.appendWhere(_ID + "=" + uri.getPathSegments().get(1));

- break;

- default:

- throw new IllegalArgumentException("Unknown URI " + uri);

- }

- if (sortOrder == null || sortOrder == ""){

- /**

- By default sort on student names

- */

- sortOrder = NAME;

- }

- Cursor c = qb.query(db, projection, selection, selectionArgs,null, null, sortOrder);

- /**

- register to watch a content URI for changes

- */

```java
c.setNotificationUri(getContext().getContentResolver(
), uri);

return c;

}


@Override

public int delete(Uri uri, String selection, String[]
selectionArgs) {

int count = 0;


switch (uriMatcher.match(uri)){

case STUDENTS:

count = db.delete(STUDENTS_TABLE_NAME,
selection, selectionArgs);

break;


case STUDENT_ID:

String id = uri.getPathSegments().get(1);
```

```
count = db.delete( STUDENTS_TABLE_NAME, _ID
+ " = " + id +

(!TextUtils.isEmpty(selection) ? " AND (" + selection
+ ')' : ""), selectionArgs);

break;



default:

throw new IllegalArgumentException("Unknown URI
" + uri);

}



getContext().getContentResolver().notifyChange(uri,
null);

return count;

}



@Override

public int update(Uri uri, ContentValues values,
String selection, String[] selectionArgs) {
```

```
• int count = 0;


• switch (uriMatcher.match(uri)){

• case STUDENTS:

• count = db.update(STUDENTS_TABLE_NAME,
  values, selection, selectionArgs);

• break;


• case STUDENT_ID:

• count = db.update(STUDENTS_TABLE_NAME,
  values, _ID + " = " + uri.getPathSegments().get(1) +

• (!TextUtils.isEmpty(selection) ? " AND (" +selection +
  ')' : ""), selectionArgs);

• break;


• default:

• throw new IllegalArgumentException("Unknown URI
  " + uri );

• }
```

- getContext().getContentResolver().notifyChange(uri, null);

- return count;

- }

- @Override

- public String getType(Uri uri) {

- switch (uriMatcher.match(uri)){

- /**

- Get all student records

- */

- case STUDENTS:

- return
"vnd.android.cursor.dir/vnd.example.students";

- /**

- Get a particular student

- */

- case STUDENT_ID:

- return
  "vnd.android.cursor.item/vnd.example.students";

- default:

- throw new IllegalArgumentException("Unsupported
  URI: " + uri);

- }

- }

- }

The next code is the modification we made to
AndroidManifest.xml to add in the <provider.../> tag,
ensuring the content provider is included:

- <?xml version="1.0" encoding="utf-8"?>

- <manifest
  xmlns:android="http://schemas.android.com/apk/re
  s/android"

- package="com.example.My Application"

- android:versionCode="1"

- android:versionName="1.0" >

- <uses-sdk

- android:minSdkVersion="8"

- android:targetSdkVersion="22" />

- <application

- android:allowBackup="true"

- android:icon="@drawable/ic_launcher"

- android:label="@string/app_name"

- android:theme="@style/AppTheme" >

- <activity

- android:name="com.example.My
  Application.MainActivity"

- android:label="@string/app_name" >

- <intent-filter>

- <action android:name="android.intent.action.MAIN" />

- <category android:name="android.intent.category.LAUNCHER" />

- </intent-filter>

- </activity>

- <provider android:name="StudentsProvider"

- <android:authorities="com.example.provider.College ">

- </provider>

- </application>

- </manifest>

The next code is the new content of the res/layout/activity_main.xml file in which we included a button that lets us broadcast our custom intents:

- <RelativeLayout xmlns:android="http://schemas.android.com/apk/res/android"

- xmlns:tools="http://schemas.android.com/tools" android:layout_width="match_parent"

- android:layout_height="match_parent" android:paddingLeft="@dimen/activity_horizontal_margin"

- android:paddingRight="@dimen/activity_horizontal_margin"

- android:paddingTop="@dimen/activity_vertical_margin"

- android:paddingBottom="@dimen/activity_vertical_margin" tools:context=".MainActivity"/">

- <TextView

- android:id="@+id/textView1"

- android:layout_width="wrap_content"

- android:layout_height="wrap_content"

- android:text="Content provider"

- android:layout_alignParentTop="true"

- android:layout_centerHorizontal="true"

- android:textSize="30dp" />

- <TextView

- android:id="@+id/textView2"

- android:layout_width="wrap_content"

- android:layout_height="wrap_content"

- android:text="Tutorials point "

- android:textColor="#ff87ff09"

- android:textSize="30dp"

- android:layout_below="@+id/textView1"

- android:layout_centerHorizontal="true" />

- <ImageButton

- android:layout_width="wrap_content"

- android:layout_height="wrap_content"

- android:id="@+id/imageButton"

- android:src="@drawable/abc"

- android:layout_below="@+id/textView2"

- android:layout_centerHorizontal="true" />

- <Button

- android:layout_width="wrap_content"

- android:layout_height="wrap_content"

- android:id="@+id/button2"

- android:text="Add Name"

- android:layout_below="@+id/editText3"

- android:layout_alignRight="@+id/textView2"

- android:layout_alignEnd="@+id/textView2"

- android:layout_alignLeft="@+id/textView2"

- android:layout_alignStart="@+id/textView2"

- android:onClick="onClickAddName"/>

- <EditText

- android:layout_width="wrap_content"

- android:layout_height="wrap_content"

- android:id="@+id/editText"

- android:layout_below="@+id/imageButton"

- android:layout_alignRight="@+id/imageButton"

- android:layout_alignEnd="@+id/imageButton" />

- <EditText

- android:layout_width="wrap_content"

- android:layout_height="wrap_content"

- android:id="@+id/editText2"

- android:layout_alignTop="@+id/editText"

- android:layout_alignLeft="@+id/textView1"

- android:layout_alignStart="@+id/textView1"

- android:layout_alignRight="@+id/textView1"

- android:layout_alignEnd="@+id/textView1"

- android:hint="Name"

- android:textColorHint="@android:color/holo_blue_l
ight" />

- <EditText

- android:layout_width="wrap_content"

- android:layout_height="wrap_content"

- android:id="@+id/editText3"

- android:layout_below="@+id/editText"

- android:layout_alignLeft="@+id/editText2"

- android:layout_alignStart="@+id/editText2"

- android:layout_alignRight="@+id/editText2"

- android:layout_alignEnd="@+id/editText2"

- android:hint="Grade"

- android:textColorHint="@android:color/holo_blue_
bright" />

- <Button

- android:layout_width="wrap_content"

- android:layout_height="wrap_content"

- android:text="Retrive student"

- android:id="@+id/button"

- android:layout_below="@+id/button2"

- android:layout_alignRight="@+id/editText3"

- android:layout_alignEnd="@+id/editText3"

- android:layout_alignLeft="@+id/button2"

- android:layout_alignStart="@+id/button2"

- android:onClick="onClickRetrieveStudents"/>

- </RelativeLayout>

Make sure that, in your res/values/strings.xml file, you have this code:

- <?xml version="1.0" encoding="utf-8"?>

- <resources>

- <string name="app_name">My Application</string>

- <string name="action_settings">Settings</string>

- </resources>;

You can now try to run the modified version of My Application. Open one of your activity files in Android Studio IDE and click the Run button in the toolbar. Provided that there are no issues, the emulator will open. Doe exercise a little patience here; if your computer is not fast, it will take time to open.

The next step is to input a Name and a Grade. Then click on the button that says Add Name and a new record will be added to the database. A message will show up at the bottom of the emulator window – the message will contain the URI and a record number. This whole operation will use the insert() method. Repeat a few more times to add more names and grades into your database.

When you have finished adding new records, you can now ask your ContentProvider for the records. Click on the button that says Retrieve Students and your records will be displayed, one at a time.

If you go into MainActivity.java, you can write new activities for the delete and update operations with callback functions and you can also modify the interface to provide new buttons for deleted and updated operations. You do this the same way that you added the buttons for the read and add operations.

By doing this, the ContentPrvider becomes something akin to an address book. Or, you can use the same concept to create applications that are database oriented, application that allow a user to do all sorts of operations, like delete, read, update and write.

Chapter 9 – Fragments

Fragments are bits of activities that provide for an activity design that is modular. A fragment could be seen as a sort of sub-activity. The following list is the most important things you need to keep in mind about fragments:

- Fragments have their own behaviors and layouts and their own life cycle callbacks

- Fragment can be removed or added in an activity while that activity is being run

- Multiple fragments can be combined in one activity in order to build up a user interface that is multi-plane

- One fragment can be used in many different activities

- The life cycle of a fragment is very closely related to that of the host activity. This means that, if the user pauses the activity, all of the fragments contained in the activity will also be paused

- Fragments are able to implement behaviors that do not have any components in the user interface

Fragments are created by extending the Fragment class. A fragment can easily be inserted into an activity layout by way of declaring it in the layout file as a <fragment> element. An application is able to embed multiple fragments into a single activity. However, if the app is being run on a tablet, only one fragment can be displayed – there is no room for any more. However, each fragment has the ability to display another when it is selected on the screen/

Life Cycle of a Fragment

Each fragment has a specific life cycle that is similar to an activity life cycle. The following are the methods that can be overwritten in the Fragment class:

- **onAttach()** – the instance associates with activity instance. Neither are completely initialized. Inside this method is usually a reference to the specific activity that is using the fragment for initialization.

- **onCreate()** – the method is called by the system when the fragment is created. The important components of the fragment that you want kept when the fragment stops or pauses and then starts must be initialized.

- **onCreateView()** - this callback is called by the system when the fragment needs to draw the interface for the very first time. In order to draw a UI, you have return a view component from the method that is the initial point of the fragment. If the fragment is not deigned to provide a UI, you may return a null

- **onActivityCreated()** - this is called after onCreateView() at the time of creating the host activity. Both the activity and the fragment instance are created along with the activity's view hierarchy. You can now access the view by calling findViewByID() method and for example, you will be able to instantiate any object that needs a Context object.

- **onStart()**- this is called as soon as the fragment is visible

- **onResume()** – this is when the fragment is active

- **onPause()** – called by the system as the initial indicator that a user is going away from the fragment. This is where changes should be committed provided they are to be in use after the user shuts down their session

- **onStop()** – called to stop the fragment

- **onDestroyView()** - calling this method will destroy the fragment view

- **onDestroy()** - called to clean up the state of the fragment. Do NOT take it for granted that the Android platform will call this method.

Creating a Fragment

There ae a set of steps that you need to go through to create a fragment:

1. Determine how many fragments are to be in one activity, i.e. perhaps you want two, one to handle landscape mode and one to handle portrait mode on the device

2. Create the classes that are needed, based on the fragments you are using. These classes are going to extend the Fragment class, which also has callback functions. Depending on your specific requirements, any of these functions can be overridden.

3. Create a layout file in the xml file, corresponding to each of the fragments. Each file will have a specific layout that is defined for a specific fragment

4. Lastly, modify your activity file so that the logic of replacing fragments is defined, again based on your needs.

Different Types of Fragment

Fragments are divided up into three separate stages:

- **Single Frame** - used for mobile hand-held device, only able to show on fragment on a view

- **List** – a fragment that contains a list view

- **Transaction - allows** one fragment to be moved to another one.

Chapter 10 – Intents and Filters

Intents are abstract descriptions of operations that are to be performed. An Intent can be used together with startActivity if an activity is to be launched, broadcastIntent if it is to be sent on to a BroadcastReceiver component, or, if it is to communicate with background services, it can be used with bindService(Intent, ServiceCommuniation, int) or startService(Intent).

Let's assume that we want to use an activity to launch an email client and that activity sends an email from your Android device. For this, you would have your activity send an ACTION_SEND, to the Intent Resolver, together with the right chooser. The chooser will provide the correct interface for the use to choose how the email data is sent:

- Intent email = new Intent(Intent.ACTION_SEND, Uri.parse("mailto:"));

- email.putExtra(Intent.EXTRA_EMAIL, recipients);

- email.putExtra(Intent.EXTRA_SUBJECT,
  subject.getText().toString());

- email.putExtra(Intent.EXTRA_TEXT,
  body.getText().toString());

- startActivity(Intent.createChooser(email, "Choose an
  email client from..."));

In this syntax, we have called startActivity to begin an activity and the result should be shown on your screen.

Next, let's assume that you want to use an activity to open a specific URL in your Android device web browser. Your activity will need to send ACTION_WEB_SEARCH to the Intent Resolver o that it will open up the specified URL in the browser. The Intent Resolver will go through a list of the activities and pic the one that matches the Intent the closest – on tis example, it would choose Web Browser Activity. The Resolver will them pas the web page on to the browser and start the activity:

- String q = "tutorialspoint";

- Intent intent = new
  Intent(Intent.ACTION_WEB_SEARCH);

- intent.putExtra(SearchManager.QUERY, q);

- startActivity(intent);

There are a number of ways that Intents can be delivered to these three types of component – Activities Broadcast receivers and Services.

Method	Description
Context.startActivity()	Intent object passed to the method to start an activity or request an activity does something different
Context.startService()	Intent object passed to the method to start a service or give a service new instructions
Context.sendBroadcast()	Intent object passed to the method to broadcast a specific message to all broadcast receivers that are interested

Intent Objects

These are information bundles used by a component that receives an Intent. The information is also used by the Android system. Intent objects may contain any of the following, based on their communication or performance needs:

Action

This is mandatory in all Intent objects. It is a string that names the specific action that is to be performed. In the case of a Broadcast Intent, the string will name the action that happened and is reported. The action will determine the structure of the rest of the Intent Object. The Intent class will define several constants that correspond to the different Intents. The action that is in the Intent class is set by using the method setAction() and it will be read by using the method getAction().

Data

This part of the object puts a data specification to a filter. The specification can be nothing more than a MIME data type, a URI or both. The URI is specified by each separate attribute of each separate part. The attributes that specify the format are both optional and mutually dependent:

- if there is no scheme specified for the filter, the rest of the URI attributes will be ignored

- if there is no host specified, the path and port attributes will be ignored

The method called setData() specifies the data as a URI; the method setType() specifies it as a MIME data type and the method setDataAndType specifies it as both. getData() is used to read the URI and getType() is used to read the data type.

Examples of some action and data pairs are:

Action and Data Pair	Description
ACTION_VIEW content://contacts/people/1	Will display all held information about the user with the specified identifier, i.e. "1"
ACTION_DIAL content://contacts/people/1	Displays the phone dialer with the specified user details shown
ACTION_VIEW tel:123	Displays the phone dialer with the specified user phone number
ACTION_DIAL tel:123	Same as above
ACTION_EDIT content://contacts/people/1	Edit the information for the person with the specified identifier
ACTION_VIEW content://contacts/people/	Displays a list of people that the user can look through
ACTION_SET_WALLPAPER	Displays the settings for choosing a new wallpaper

ACTION_SYNC	will occur at the same time as data.constant value android.intent.action.SYNC
ACTION_SYSTEM_TUTORIAL	Starts the tutorial that is either set for startup or defined by the platform
ACTION_TIMEZONE_CHANGED	Advise when the time zone alters
ACTION_UNINSTALL_PACKAGE	Runs the default uninstaller

Category

This is an optional part to the object. It is a string that contains extra information about the sort of component that can handle the Intent. We use the addCategory() method to put a category into an Intent object, the method removeCategory() to delete one that has already been added and the method getCategories() to show all the categories that are in the object.

Extras

Key-value pairs that contain extra information that is to be sent to the component that handles the Intent. These can be set using the method putExtras() and read with the method getExtras().

Flags

Flags are also optional and are used to tell the system how it should launch a specific activity and how to treat that activity once it has been launched.

Flags	Description
FLAG_ACTIVITY_CLEAR_TASK	When set in the Intent that is passed to Context.startActivity(), will case exiting associated tasks to be cleared before the activity begins.
FLAG_ACTIVITY_CLEAR_TOP	If the launched activity is running in the task and this flag is set, all instance of the activity will be closed down before a new one is opened.
FLAG_ACTIVITY_NEW_TASK	Used by an activity that requires to present a behavior in the style of a launcher The user is provided with a list of activities which will run independently of the launching activity

Component Name

This is also an optional field in the object and is a ComponentName object that represents Service, Activity or BroadcastReceiver classes. If set, the object will be sent to an instant of the specified class; if none is specified, the system will use alternative information that is in the Intent object to find another target that is deemed suitable. It is set by using the method setComponent(), setClassName() or setClass() and is read by using the method getComponent().

Different Types of Intent

Android supports two types of Intents:

- **Explicit Intents**

These are intents that connect the applications together internally. Let's say that you wanted to connect an activity to another, you would use an explicit intent to do it. The Intent specifies the component being targeted by name. These Intents are usually used for internal message, like activities that launch sister or subordinate activities. An example of this is:

- // Explicit Intent by specifying its class name

- Intent i = new Intent(FirstActivity.this, SecondAcitivity.class);

- // Starts TargetActivity

- startActivity(i);

- **Implicit Intents**

An implicit intent does not specify a target by name and the component field is left empty. These are usually used to activate a component that is in a different application. An example of this:

- Intent read1=new Intent();

- read1.setAction(android.content.Intent.ACTION_VIE W);

- read1.setData(ContactsContract.Contacts.CONTENT_ URI);

- startActivity(read1);

The component being targeted, the one that actually receives the intent can make use of the method getExtras() to grab the data that is being sent. For example:

- // Get bundle object at appropriate place in your code

- Bundle extras = getIntent().getExtras();

- // Extract data using passed keys

- String value1 = extras.getString("Key1");

- String value2 = extras.getString("Key2");

The following shows you how an Intent functions to launch different built-in applications.

Step	Description
1	Use Android Studio IDE to make a new application called My Application. This is done under the package called com.example.saira_000.myapplication. When you create this, ensure that use the latest Android SDK to Target SDK and Compile With so that you get the latest APIs
2	Now change src/main/java/MainActivity.java to include two listeners with corresponding buttons called Start Phone and Start Browser
3	Change res/layout/activity_main.xml to include three linear layout buttons
4	Run the modified application so the emulator opens and check the results.

The following is the modified content of src/com.example.My Application/MainActivity.java:

- package com.example.saira_000.myapplication;

- import android.content.Intent;

- import android.net.Uri;

- import android.support.v7.app.ActionBarActivity;

- import android.os.Bundle;

- import android.view.Menu;

- import android.view.MenuItem;

- import android.view.View;

- import android.widget.Button;

- public class MainActivity extends ActionBarActivity {

- Button b1,b2;

- @Override

- protected void onCreate(Bundle savedInstanceState) {

- super.onCreate(savedInstanceState);

- setContentView(R.layout.activity_main);

- b1=(Button)findViewById(R.id.button);

- b1.setOnClickListener(new View.OnClickListener() {

- @Override

- public void onClick(View v) {

- Intent i = new Intent(android.content.Intent.ACTION_VIEW, Uri.parse("http://www.example.com"));

- startActivity(i);

- }

- });

- b2=(Button)findViewById(R.id.button2);

- b2.setOnClickListener(new View.OnClickListener() {

- @Override

- public void onClick(View v) {

- Intent i = new Intent(android.content.Intent.ACTION_VIEW,Uri.parse("tel:9510300000"));

- startActivity(i);

- }

- });

- }

- @Override

- public boolean onCreateOptionsMenu(Menu menu) {

- // Inflate the menu; this adds items to the action bar if it is present.

- getMenuInflater().inflate(R.menu.menu_main, menu);

- return true;

- }

- @Override

- public boolean onOptionsItemSelected(MenuItem item) {

- // Handle action bar item clicks here. The action bar will

- // automatically handle clicks on the Home/Up button, so long

- // as you specify a parent activity in AndroidManifest.xml.

- int id = item.getItemId();

- //noinspection SimplifiableIfStatement

- if (id == R.id.action_settings) {

- return true;

- }

- return super.onOptionsItemSelected(item);

- }

- }

The next is the new content for res/layout/activity_main.xml:

- <RelativeLayout xmlns:android="http://schemas.android.com/apk/res/android"

- xmlns:tools="http://schemas.android.com/tools"

- android:layout_width="match_parent"

- android:layout_height="match_parent"

- android:paddingLeft="@dimen/activity_horizontal_margin"

- android:paddingRight="@dimen/activity_horizontal_margin"

- android:paddingTop="@dimen/activity_vertical_margin"

- android:paddingBottom="@dimen/activity_vertical_margin"

- tools:context=".MainActivity">

- <TextView

- android:id="@+id/textView1"

- android:layout_width="wrap_content"

- android:layout_height="wrap_content"

- android:text="Intent Example"

- android:layout_alignParentTop="true"

- android:layout_centerHorizontal="true"

- android:textSize="30dp" />

- <TextView

- android:id="@+id/textView2"

- android:layout_width="wrap_content"

- android:layout_height="wrap_content"

- android:text="Tutorials point"

- android:textColor="#ff87ff09"

- android:textSize="30dp"

- android:layout_below="@+id/textView1"

- android:layout_centerHorizontal="true" />

- <ImageButton

- android:layout_width="wrap_content"

- android:layout_height="wrap_content"

- android:id="@+id/imageButton"

- android:src="@drawable/abc"

- android:layout_below="@+id/textView2"

- android:layout_centerHorizontal="true" />

- <EditText

- android:layout_width="wrap_content"

- android:layout_height="wrap_content"

- android:id="@+id/editText"

- android:layout_below="@+id/imageButton"

- android:layout_alignRight="@+id/imageButton"

- android:layout_alignEnd="@+id/imageButton" />

- <Button

- android:layout_width="wrap_content"

- android:layout_height="wrap_content"

- android:text="Start Browser"

- android:id="@+id/button"

- android:layout_alignTop="@+id/editText"

- android:layout_alignRight="@+id/textView1"

- android:layout_alignEnd="@+id/textView1"

- android:layout_alignLeft="@+id/imageButton"

- android:layout_alignStart="@+id/imageButton" />

- <Button

- android:layout_width="wrap_content"

- android:layout_height="wrap_content"

- android:text="Start Phone"

- android:id="@+id/button2"

- android:layout_below="@+id/button"

- android:layout_alignLeft="@+id/button"

- android:layout_alignStart="@+id/button"

- android:layout_alignRight="@+id/textView2"

- android:layout_alignEnd="@+id/textView2" />

- </RelativeLayout>

This next set of code is the modification made to res/values/strings.xml, defining the new constants:

- <?xml version="1.0" encoding="utf-8"?>

- <resources>

- <string name="app_name">My Applicaiton</string>

- <string name="action_settings">Settings</string>

- </resources>

This is the AndroidManifest.xml file containing the default content:

- <?xml version="1.0" encoding="utf-8"?>

- <manifest xmlns:android="http://schemas.android.com/apk/res/android"

- package="com.example.My Application"

- android:versionCode="1"

- android:versionName="1.0" >

- <uses-sdk

- android:minSdkVersion="8"

- android:targetSdkVersion="22" />

- <application

- android:allowBackup="true"

- android:icon="@drawable/ic_launcher"

- android:label="@string/app_name"

- android:theme="@style/AppTheme" >

- <activity

- android:name="com.example.saira_000.myapplicati
  on.MainActivity"

- android:label="@string/app_name" >

- <intent-filter>

- <action android:name="android.intent.action.MAIN" />

- <category android:name="android.intent.category.LAUNCHER" />

- </intent-filter>

- </activity>

- </application>

- </manifest>

Now run the modified version of My Application by opening Android Studio, opening a project activity file and then clicking Run. If all is well, the emulator will open.

Click the button that says Start Browser and you will see a browser open up already configured with http://example.com

Click the button that says Start Phone and you can dial the number that shows up

Intent Filters

You know how an Intent is used to call an activity. Android also makes use of filters to highlight the Activities, Broadcast Receivers and Services that are able to handle the Intent, with the use of specified and associated data, actions, and categories. You should use the element <intent filter> in the manifest file so that you can list all the categories, actions and data types associated with the services, activities and broadcast receivers.

The following example is part of the AndroidManifest.xml file, showing com.example.My Application.CustomActivity being specified and which can be invoked with one of the two actions mentioned, one data and one category:

- <activity android:name=".CustomActivity"

- android:label="@string/app_name">

- <intent-filter>

- <action android:name="android.intent.action.VIEW" />

- <action android:name="com.example.My Application.LAUNCH" />

- <category android:name="android.intent.category.DEFAULT" />

- <data android:scheme="http" />

- </intent-filter>

- </activity>

When this activity has been defined, together with the filters, it can be invoked by other activities that use one of the following — android.intent.action.VIEW or com.example.My Appliation.LAUNCH, so long as they have the category android.intent.category.DEFAULT.

<data> is used to specify which data type the activity will call for and, as you can see from the above, the custom activity is looking for the data to be defined with http://.

The following are checks that are performed by Android before an activity is invoked:

- A filter may list several actions but cannot be empty. The filter must have at least one action in it otherwise all Intents will be blocked. When there is more than one listed, the system will attempt to match one before the activity can be invoked

- Filter can have many categories. If there are none, the system will pass on this test but when there is more than one, every category mentioned in the object has to match with a category that is listed in the filter. If they don't, the intent cannot pass the category test

- <data> elements can have a data type and a URI. There are several attributes for each separate part of the URI, including host, port scheme and path. If an Intent object as both a data type and a URI the data type has to match a data type that is in the filter in order to pass the test.

The following shows you a modification of the example we used above. You will be shown how the system resolves a conflict when one intent tries to invoke two activities, how to invoke custom activities by using filters and an exception in the event that the system does not file the right activity definition for a specific intent.

Step	Description
1	Use Android Studio IDE to make an application called My Application. This will be under the package named com.example.saira_ooo.myapplication

2	Next change src/Main/Java/MainActivty.java by adding in the code that will define three listeners, each of which corresponds to a button that is defined in the layout file
3	Next, make a new src/Main/Java/CustomActivity.java file that has a single custom activity that can be invoked by a number of intents
4	Change res/layout/activity_main.xml so that three buttons in linear are added
5	Make a new res/layout/custom_view.xml file that includes a <TextView> that shows the data passed through the intent
6	Change AndroidManifest.xml to include an <intent-filter> that defines the rules that the intent follows to invoke the custom activity
7	Run the modified application to open the emulator and check on the results.

The following is the modified code for src/MainActivity.java:

- package com.example.saira_000.myapplication;

- import android.content.Intent;

- import android.net.Uri;

- import android.support.v7.app.ActionBarActivity;

- import android.os.Bundle;

- import android.view.Menu;

- import android.view.MenuItem;

- import android.view.View;

- import android.widget.Button;

- public class MainActivity extends ActionBarActivity {

- Button b1,b2,b3;

- @Override

- protected void onCreate(Bundle savedInstanceState) {

- super.onCreate(savedInstanceState);

- setContentView(R.layout.activity_main);

- b1=(Button)findViewById(R.id.button);

- b1.setOnClickListener(new View.OnClickListener() {

- @Override

- public void onClick(View v) {

- Intent i = new Intent(android.content.Intent.ACTION_VIEW,Uri.parse("http://www.example.com"));

- startActivity(i);

- }

- });

- b2=(Button)findViewById(R.id.button2);

- b2.setOnClickListener(new View.OnClickListener() {

- @Override

- public void onClick(View v) {

- Intent i = new Intent("com.example.My Application.LAUNCH",Uri.parse("http://www.example.com"));

- startActivity(i);

- }

- });

- b3=(Button)findViewById(R.id.button3);

- b3.setOnClickListener(new View.OnClickListener() {

- @Override

- public void onClick(View v) {

- Intent i = new Intent("com.example.My Application.LAUNCH",Uri.parse("https://www.example.com"));

- startActivity(i);

- }

- });

- }

- @Override

- public boolean onCreateOptionsMenu(Menu menu) {

- // Inflate the menu; this adds items to the action bar if it is present.

- getMenuInflater().inflate(R.menu.menu_main, menu);

- return true;

- }

- @Override

- public boolean onOptionsItemSelected(MenuItem item) {

- // Handle action bar item clicks here. The action bar will

- // automatically handle clicks on the Home/Up button, so long

- // as you specify a parent activity in AndroidManifest.xml.

- int id = item.getItemId();

- //noinspection SimplifiableIfStatement

- if (id == R.id.action_settings) {

- return true;

- }

- return super.onOptionsItemSelected(item);

- }

- }

The next code is the modified content of src/com.example.My Application/CustomActivity.java:

- package com.example.saira_ooo.myapplication;

- import android.app.Activity;

- import android.net.Uri;

- import android.os.Bundle;

- import android.widget.TextView;

- public class CustomActivity extends Activity {

- @Override

- public void onCreate(Bundle savedInstanceState) {

- super.onCreate(savedInstanceState);

- setContentView(R.layout.custom_view);

- TextView label = (TextView) findViewById(R.id.show_data);

- Uri url = getIntent().getData();

- label.setText(url.toString());

- }

- }

Next, we have the code for res/layout/activity_main.xml:

- <RelativeLayout xmlns:android="http://schemas.android.com/apk/res/android"

- xmlns:tools="http://schemas.android.com/tools"

- android:layout_width="match_parent"

- android:layout_height="match_parent"

- android:paddingLeft="@dimen/activity_horizontal_margin"

- android:paddingRight="@dimen/activity_horizontal_margin"

- android:paddingTop="@dimen/activity_vertical_margin"

- android:paddingBottom="@dimen/activity_vertical_margin"

- tools:context=".MainActivity">

- <TextView

- android:id="@+id/textView1"

- android:layout_width="wrap_content"

- android:layout_height="wrap_content"

- android:text="Intent Example"

- android:layout_alignParentTop="true"

- android:layout_centerHorizontal="true"

- android:textSize="30dp" />

- <TextView

- android:id="@+id/textView2"

- android:layout_width="wrap_content"

- android:layout_height="wrap_content"

- android:text="Tutorials point"

- android:textColor="#ff87ff09"

- android:textSize="30dp"

- android:layout_below="@+id/textView1"

- android:layout_centerHorizontal="true" />

- <ImageButton

- android:layout_width="wrap_content"

- android:layout_height="wrap_content"

- android:id="@+id/imageButton"

- android:src="@drawable/abc"

- android:layout_below="@+id/textView2"

- android:layout_centerHorizontal="true" />

- \<EditText

- android:layout_width="wrap_content"

- android:layout_height="wrap_content"

- android:id="@+id/editText"

- android:layout_below="@+id/imageButton"

- android:layout_alignRight="@+id/imageButton"

- android:layout_alignEnd="@+id/imageButton" />

- \<Button

- android:layout_width="wrap_content"

- android:layout_height="wrap_content"

- android:text="Start browsing with view action"

- android:id="@+id/button"

- android:layout_alignTop="@+id/editText"

- android:layout_alignRight="@+id/textView1"

- android:layout_alignEnd="@+id/textView1"

- android:layout_alignLeft="@+id/imageButton"

- android:layout_alignStart="@+id/imageButton" />

- <Button

- android:layout_width="wrap_content"

- android:layout_height="wrap_content"

- android:text="Start browsing with launch action"

- android:id="@+id/button2"

- android:layout_below="@+id/button"

- android:layout_alignLeft="@+id/button"

- android:layout_alignStart="@+id/button"

- android:layout_alignRight="@+id/textView2"

- android:layout_alignEnd="@+id/textView2" />

- <Button

- android:layout_width="wrap_content"

- android:layout_height="wrap_content"

- android:text="Exceptional condition"

- android:id="@+id/button3"

- android:layout_below="@+id/button2"

- android:layout_alignLeft="@+id/button2"

- android:layout_alignStart="@+id/button2"

- android:layout_alignRight="@+id/textView2"

- android:layout_alignEnd="@+id/textView2" />

- </RelativeLayout>

Then we have the code for res/layout/custom_view.xml:

- <?xml version="1.0" encoding="utf-8"?>

- <LinearLayout
  xmlns:android="http://schemas.android.com/apk/re
  s/android"

- android:orientation="vertical"

- android:layout_width="fill_parent"

- android:layout_height="fill_parent">

- <TextView android:id="@+id/show_data"

- android:layout_width="fill_parent"

- android:layout_height="400dp"/>

- </LinearLayout>

And the content of res/values/strings.xml including the definitions for two constants:

- <?xml version="1.0" encoding="utf-8"?>

- <resources>

- <string name="app_name">My Application</string>

- <string name="action_settings">Settings</string>

- </resources>

Lastly, we have the content of AndroidManifest.xml:

- <?xml version="1.0" encoding="utf-8"?>

- <manifest xmlns:android="http://schemas.android.com/apk/res/android"

- package="com.example.My Application"

- android:versionCode="1"

- android:versionName="1.0" >

- <uses-sdk

- android:minSdkVersion="8"

- android:targetSdkVersion="22" />

- <application

- android:allowBackup="true"

- android:icon="@drawable/ic_launcher"

- android:label="@string/app_name"

- android:theme="@style/AppTheme" >

- <activity

- android:name="com.example.saira_000.myapplicati on"

- android:label="@string/app_name" >

- <intent-filter>

- `<action android:name="android.intent.action.MAIN" />`

- `<category android:name="android.intent.category.LAUNCHER" />`

- `</intent-filter>`

- `</activity>`

- `<activity android:name="com.example.saira_000.myapplication.CustomActivity"`

- `<android:label="@string/app_name">`

- `<intent-filter>`

- `<action android:name="android.intent.action.VIEW" />`

- `<action android:name="com.example.saira_000.myapplication.LAUNCH" />`

- <category android:name="android.intent.category.DEFAULT" />

- <data android:scheme="http" />

- </intent-filter>

- </activity>

- </application>

- </manifest>

Now you can run the modified version of your My Application file, containing all these new changes. As usual, open the project activity and click run wait for the application to install in your AVD and, if all is good, you will see the emulator.

Begin by clicking on Start Browser with VIEW Action. You defined this custom activity with the android.intent.action.VIEW filter and, as there is a default activity already shown against the VIEW action, defined to launch the web browser by Android, you should see two options to choose from, both of them activities.

If you click on Browser, the web browser will open in example.com but if you were to click on IntentDemo, the Custom activity would be launched. This only passed data that has been captured and displays it as text.

Use the Back button and then click Start Browser with LAUNCH Action. A filter is applied and your chosen activity will be launched.

Use the Back button again and, this time, click on Exception Condition. Android will now look for a filter that is valid for the intent. It won't find any valid activity because we used https for the data instead of http.

Chapter 11 – User Interface Layouts

View is the most basic of all the building blocks for the user interface. This is an object created from View lass and it sits in an area of the screen, rectangle in shape, with the responsibility for handling event and drawing. It is the base class for the widgets and these are used for creating components that are interactive, like text fields, buttons, etc.

ViewGroup is a subclass of View and it has a container that is invisible. This container stores other ViewGroups or Views and it defines the properties of their layouts. There are a few different layouts that are also subclasses of ViewGroup. The usual layout is used to define how the user interface is structured visually and it can be created using the View and/or ViewGroup objects at runtime or the layout can be declared with an xml file called main_layout.xml. You will find this in the res/layout folder inside your project.

I am going to try to keep this tutorial simple and make it about using the xml file to create your GUI layouts. You can include widgets, like labels, buttons, textboxes and many others besides. The following example shows you a simple xml file that has linear layout.

- <?xml version="1.0" encoding="utf-8"?>

- <LinearLayout xmlns:android="http://schemas.android.com/apk/res/android"

- android:layout_width="fill_parent"

- android:layout_height="fill_parent"

- android:orientation="vertical" >

- <TextView android:id="@+id/text"

- android:layout_width="wrap_content"

- android:layout_height="wrap_content"

- android:text="This is a TextView" />

- <Button android:id="@+id/button"

- android:layout_width="wrap_content"

- android:layout_height="wrap_content"

- android:text="This is a Button" />

- <!-- More GUI components go here -->

- </LinearLayout>

When you have made your layout, call the Activity.onCreate() method to load the layout resource, as in the following example:

- public void onCreate(Bundle savedInstanceState) {

- super.onCreate(savedInstanceState);

- setContentView(R.layout.activity_main);

- }

Types of Android Layout

Android contains a few different layout types and these will be used in virtually every Android application, according to the look and the feel you want to create with your app:

Layout Type	Description
Linear Layout	This is a ViewGroup that aligns in one direction, horizontally or vertically
Relative Layout	ViewGroup that displays the views in relative positions
Table Layout	ViewGroup the shows the views grouped into columns and rows
Absolute Layout	Lets you specify an exact location
Frame Layout	A screen placeholder that allows you to show one single view
List View	ViewGroup that shows scrollable items in a list
Grid View	ViewGroup that shows items in a scrollable grid that is two-dimensional

Layout Attributes

Each separate layout has its own attributes and it is these that define how the layout looks visually. All the layouts contain common attributes and there are also other attributes that are specific to certain layouts. These are the most common attributes and these are applied to every layout:

Attribute	Description
android:id	The ID that identifies the view
android:layout_width	Layout width
android:layout_height	Layout height
android:layout_marginTop	The empty space at the top of the layout
android:layout_marginBottom	The empty space at the bottom of the layout
android:layout_marginLeft	The empty space at the left of the layout
android:layout_marginRight	The empty space at the right of the layout
android:layout_marginRight	Specified the positioning of child Views
android:layout_weight	Defines how the empty space should be allocated to the View

android:layout_x	The x-co-ordinate of the specific layout
android:layout_y	The y co-ordinate of the specific layout
android:layout_width	The layout width
android:paddingLeft	The filler for the left padding on the layout
android:paddingRight	The filler for the right padding on the layout
android:paddingTop	The filler for the top padding on the layout
android:paddingBottom	The filler for the bottom padding on the layout

The width and the height are the layout dimensions and these are specified in either:

- dp – Density-Independent Pixels

- sp – Scale-Independent Pixels

- pt – Points which are equal to 1 72 of an inch

- px – Pixels

- mm – Millimeters

- in – Inches

You can use exact measurements to specify the height and the width of your layout but, in most cases, you will probably use one of the following constants to set your height and width:

- **android:layout_width=wrap_content** –   this orders the View to set is own size, dependent on the dimensions that the content requires

- **android:layout_width=fill_parent** – Order the view to size itself to the size of the parent view

One thing that plays a vital role in the positioning of a view object is gravity attributes. It can take any of the following constants and, if it takes more than one, they are separated by a |:

Constant	Value	Description
top	0 x 30	Does not change the size, it pushes the object up to the top of the container
bottom	0 x 50	Does not change the size, it pushes the object to the bottom of the container

left	0 x 03	Does not change the size, it pushes the object to the left of the container
right	0 x 05	Does not change the size, it pushes the object to the right of the container
center_vertical	0 x 10	Puts an object into the vertical center of the container but does not change its size
fill_vertical	0 x 70	Enlarge the object if requires until it fills up the container fully
center_horizontal	0 x 01	Puts the object into the horizontal center of the container but does into change its size
fill_horizontal	0 x 07	Enlarges the object of requires to fill the container completely
center	0 x 11	Puts the object into the center of the container, using the horizontal and vertical axis but does not

		change its size
fill	0 x 77	Enlarges the object horizontally and vertically to fill the container completely
clip_vertical	0 x 80	This is an extra option that allows the bottom and/or top edges to be clipped to be within the bounds of the container. The clip is based on vertical gravity – bottom gravity clips the top, top gravity clips the bottom and neither clips both edges
clip_horizontal	0 x 08	As above but based on horizontal gravity – right gravity clips the left, left gravity clips the right and neither clips both edges
start	0 x 00800003	Pushes the object to the start of the container but does not change its size
end	0 x 00800005	Pushes the object to the end of the container but does not change its size

View Identification

View objects are assigned with unique IDs, which are used to enable the view to be identified within the tree. The ID syntax, which is in an xml tag, is:

- android:id="@+id/my_button"

Chapter 12 – UI Controls

The input controls on an application are the components of the user interface that your users interact with. Android supplies a large number of different controls that can be used in the interface, including text fields, buttons, seek bars, zoom buttons, check boxes, toggle buttons and many more besides.

Views are objects that draw on the device screen. What they draw is what the user interacts with. A ViewGroup is the object that contains the View objects that define the user interface layout.

Your layout s defined inside an xml file, which offers up a structure that is readable by the human eye, similar to an html file. For example, if you were to define a vertical layout that had a button and a text view, it would look like this:

- `<?xml version="1.0" encoding="utf-8"?>`

- `<LinearLayout xmlns:android="http://schemas.android.com/apk/res/android"`

- `android:layout_width="fill_parent"`

- `android:layout_height="fill_parent"`

- `android:orientation="vertical" >`

- `<TextView android:id="@+id/text"`

- `android:layout_width="wrap_content"`

- `android:layout_height="wrap_content"`

- `android:text="I am a TextView" />`

- `<Button android:id="@+id/button"`

- `android:layout_width="wrap_content"`

- `android:layout_height="wrap_content"`

- `android:text="I am a Button" />`

- </LinearLayout>

Android UI Controls

Android also provides a range of UI controls and these are used to help build up the graphical interface in your application.

UI Control	Description
TextView	This is what displays the test to a user
EditText	A pre-defined subclass that has the capability for rich-text editing
AutoCompleteTextView	Similar t the above but this one displays a list of autocomplete suggestions when the user starts typing
Button	Push button that the user can click or tap to carry out an action
ImageButton	Uses AbsoluteLayout to specify the exact location of the child or children
CheckBox	A switch that the user can toggle on or off. This should be in use when you are giving your users a group of options to choose from, especially those that are not mutually exclusive

ToggleButton	A toggle switch for on and off that has a light indicator
RadioButton	Has two different states – unchecked and checked
RadioGroup	Used to group together RadioButtons
ProgressBar	Provides a user with a visual feedback on the progress of tasks, i.e. if a task is being run in the background
Spinner	Drop down menu that users can select from
TimePicker	Allows a user to choose a specific time, in 12 or 24-hour mode
DatePicker	Allows users to select a date

How to Create a UI Control

If you want to create a UI Control, View or Widget, you need to define the view or widget in the layout file. You then need to give it a unique code:

- <?xml version="1.0" encoding="utf-8"?>

- <LinearLayout
  xmlns:android="http://schemas.android.com/apk/res/android"

- android:layout_width="fill_parent"

- android:layout_height="fill_parent"

- android:orientation="vertical" >

- <TextView android:id="@+id/text_id"

- android:layout_width="wrap_content"

- android:layout_height="wrap_content"

- android:text="I am a TextView" />

- </LinearLayout>

Lastly, create the instance of the control object and use the following syntax to capture it from the layout:

- TextView myText = (TextView)
findViewById(R.id.text_id);

Conclusion

As you can see, app development for the Android platform isn't too difficult, but you do have to put in the time on learning how to program and on getting to grips with all the different components. To be fair, the Android SDK and Eclipse are user-friendly and you shouldn't have too much trouble in getting your first app developed and ready for the market.

RECOMMENDED READING

Android: App Development & Programming Guide: Learn In A Day!

hyperurl.co/androids

Hacking: Hacking For Beginners and Basic Security: How To Hack

hyperurl.co/hacking

Internet Security: Online Protection From Computer Hacking

hyperurl.co/security

Programming Swift: Create A Fully Functioning App: Learn In A Day!

hyperurl.co/swift